# GLOBAL MANIA!

Take a trivia trip through the ages and around the world. TRIVIA MANIA is your ticket to such brain-stumpers as:

— Who was the Republican Party's first president?
— What was the leaders' motto in the French Revolution?
— What was Winston Churchill's World War II naval rank?
— The Principality of Andorra is between what two countries?
— What is Ireland's longest river?
— Whose assassination at Sarajevo triggered World War I?
— On which Hawaiian island is Pearl Harbor?
— Where is the world's driest spot?
— How many people were executed at the Salem witch hunt?
— The Soviet Union covers what fraction of the world's land surface?

For answers to these and more than 1000 other fascinating questions, keep on reading and surrender yourself to TRIVIA MANIA!

## TRIVIA MANIA
by Xavier Einstein

TRIVIA MANIA has arrived! With enough questions to answer every trivia buff's dreams, TRIVIA MANIA covers it all—from the delightfully obscure to the seemingly obvious. Tickle your fancy, and test your memory!

# HISTORY & GEOGRAPHY

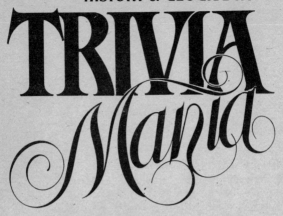

## TRIVIA Mania

XAVIER EINSTEIN

**ZEBRA BOOKS**
**KENSINGTON PUBLISHING CORP.**

ZEBRA BOOKS

are published by

Kensington Publishing Corp.
475 Park Avenue South
New York, N.Y. 10016

First printing: June, 1984

Printed in the United States of America

# TRIVIA MANIA:
## *History and Geography*

1) What was Winston Churchill's World War II naval rank?

2) Who sent the brief message "I came, I saw, I conquered"?

3) What Canadian city has the Stampede?

4) Wife of Napoleon III?

5) Which Scottish king is associated with a spider?

6) The Island of Bikini is in which island group?

7) What was the name of the punitive cell, 15 by 18 feet, into which Suraja Dowla in 1765 ordered 146 Europeans kept overnight, of which 23 still lived in the morning?

8) In what war did a wounded American naval officer shout, "Don't give up the ship!"

# . . . Answers

1. First Lord of the Admiralty

2. Julius Caesar

3. Calgary

4. Empress Eugénie

5. Robert Bruce

6. Marshall Islands

7. The Black Hole of Calcutta

8. The War of 1812, in a battle between the American *Chesapeake* and British *Shannon* outside Boston Harbor

# QUESTIONS

9) What state is known as the Pine Tree State?

10) Who was the leader of the Hungarian revolt against Soviet domination?

11) What American general said, "War is hell!"?

12) What is the hottest ever place in North America?

13) How many wives did Henry VIII have executed in the Tower of London?

14) When was Franklin D. Roosevelt stricken with polio?

15) The Principality of Andorra is between what two countries?

16) What was Hannibal doing with elephants in the Alps?

17) Into what three estates was medieval society divided?

18) Capital city of Laos?

19) What is the largest bay on the Alabama coast?

20) What famed historian claimed that history is a record of "little more than the crimes, follies, and misfortunes of mankind"?

# . . . Answers

9. Maine

10. Imre Nagy

11. William Tecumseh Sherman

12. Death Valley, Calif., with 134 degrees

13. Two, Anne Boleyn and Catherine Howard

14. August 1921

15. Spain and France

16. They were part of the army he marched from Spain by land into Italy to attack Rome

17. First estate: nobles; second estate: clergy; third estate: peasants

18. Vientiane

19. Mobile Bay

20. Edward Gibbon

# QUESTIONS

21) Who was the Republican Party's first candidate for U.S. president?

22) What were the ordinary people of ancient Rome called?

23) Straits at Istanbul?

24) Which king was executed during the French Revolution?

25) What is the name of the medieval system of allegiance and land distribution?

26) Highest point in Montana?

27) How many American troops lost their lives in World War I?
    a. 112,432                   b. 149,413

28) What was the name of the daughter of the Virginia chief Powhatan that married John Rolfe?

29) State capital of Minnesota?

30) Who was Abraham Lincoln's running mate in the 1860 presidential election?

31) What year was Florida purchased by the United States?
    a. 1801         c. 1819
    b. 1805        d. 1823

# . . . Answers

21. John C. Fremont

22. Plebs or plebeians

23. Bosphorus

24. Louis XVI

25. Feudalism

26. Granite Peak

27. a

28. Pocahontas

29. St. Paul

30. Hannibal Hamlin

31. c

32) What Midwestern state is said to have more covered bridges than Vermont?

33) Christopher Columbus was from what Italian city?

34) Which German president was pressured into appointing Hitler chancellor in 1933?

35) Austria is slightly smaller than:
    a. New York State
    b. Maine
    c. West Virginia

36) Mesopotamian civilizations depended on what two great rivers?

37) Who led the Normans to victory in the Battle of Hastings?

38) What Caribbean island is east of Curaçao?

39) What is the popular name of the Florida Everglades Parkway from Naples to Fort Lauderdale?

40) Who unified 19th century Germany through "blood and iron"?

41) From what European nation did America buy its Virgin Islands in 1916?

42) What active duty did the six Vestal Virgins perform in ancient Rome?

# . . . Answers

32. Ohio

33. Genoa

34. Von Hindenburg

35. b

36. Tigris and Euphrates

37. William the Conqueror

38. Bonaire

39. Alligator Alley

40. Bismarck

41. Denmark

42. They kept the sacred fire burning in the Temple of Vesta

# QUESTIONS

43) What is the name of the sea between Scandinavia and the European continent?

44) What was Napoleon's first defeat by Nelson?

45) Since Jefferson was a widower, who became unofficial first lady during his administration and official first lady during the next?

46) What two mountain ranges have all the world's highest mountains?

47) Approximately how many people perished in Stalin's purges during the 1930s?
    a. 1 million
    b. 5 million
    c. 10 million
    d. 15 million

48) How many colonies were involved in the American Revolution?

49) What state is known as the Battle Born State?

50) America's oldest standing synagogue?

51) Who killed Abraham Lincoln?

52) On what river is Vienna built?

53) The War of the Roses was fought between which two English royal houses?

# . . . _Answers_

43. Baltic

44. The Battle of the Nile

45. Dolly Madison

46. Himalayas and Karakoram

47. c

48. 13

49. Nevada

50. Touro Synagogue, Newport, RI

51. John Wilkes Booth

52. Danube

53. The House of York and the House of Lancaster

54) Name of Rumanian fascist party?

55) What fraction of the land surface of China is under cultivation?

56) Which came first, the ancient Hittites or Assyrians?

57) The military orders of the Hospitallers, Templars and Teutonic Knights originated from what armed expeditions?

58) What state is known as the Land of Opportunity?

59) What 19th century British general was killed by Muslim radicals at Khartoum?

60) Which two states enclose Chesapeake Bay?

61) What was the collective name for the classified documents on U.S. involvement in Vietnam which the New York Times published in 1971?

62) What river did Julius Caesar cross with his army, signifying his refusal to disband his soldiers?

63) What are the mountains between France and Spain named?

64) Russia on one side, and Turkey, Britain and France on the other, fought what war?

# . . . *Answers*

54. Iron Guard

55. One-tenth

56. Hittites

57. The Crusades

58. Arkansas

59. Gordon

60. Maryland and Virginia

61. The Pentagon Papers

62. Rubicon

63. Pyrenees

64. Crimean War

65) When told that the people had no bread, what queen of France replied, "Let them eat cake"?

66) Where is Fingal's Cave?

67) Who was head of Irish rebel intelligence against the British and originator of many espionage techniques?
   a. Padraic Pearse
   b. James Connolly
   c. Michael Collins
   d. W. B. Yeats

68) What two men led the American delegation to Paris to make peace with Britain and conclude the American Revolution?

69) State capital of North Carolina?

70) What was the name of the American ship sunk by a mine in Havana habor, causing the Spanish-American war?

71) In what American city are the twin trapezoidal towers of Pennzoil Place?

72) Beyond national loyalties, who were opposed in the Thirty Years War?

73) On what river is Cairo built?

74) Date of German invasion of Poland, and date of Britain and France's declaration of war on Germany?

# . . . *Answers*

65. Marie Antoinette

66. Western Scotland, on island of Staffa

67. c

68. Benjamin Franklin and John Adams

69. Raleigh

70. USS *Maine*

71. Houston

72. Catholics vs. Protestants

73. Nile

74. Invasion, Sept. 1, 1939; war declared, Sept. 3, 1939

75) Who created the biggest empire of the ancient world, extending from Greece to India, and died at the age of 32?

76) What great river forms part of the border between Hungary and Czechoslovakia?

77) Stirrups could be said to be one of the greatest innovations of medieval warfare because they allowed the mounted rider to do what?

78) State capital of Illinois?

79) Other name for the Indian Mutiny?

80) In which state is the Black Rock Desert?

81) In what year was the European Common Market established?

82) Name of the elite bodyguard of the Roman emperor?

83) What Pacific gulf lies between El Salvador, Honduras and Nicaragua?

84) Where was the Batavian Republic (1795–1806)?

85) Who was Nazi ambassador to Austria and Turkey, later acquitted at the Nuremberg trials?

# . . . Answers

75. Alexander the Great

76. Danube

77. Put the force of his galloping horse behind a lance

78. Springfield

79. The Sepoy Rebellion

80. Nevada

81. 1957

82. The Praetorian Guard

83. Gulf of Fonseca

84. The Netherlands

85. Franz von Papen

86) How long is the border between Canada and the 48 conterminous states, including the Great Lakes?
   a. 3987 miles
   b. 4046
   c. 4324
   d. 4714

87) What was the name of the international unit formed to fight Franco in the Spanish Civil War?

88) What state is known as the Keystone State?

89) What was the name of Teddy Roosevelt's volunteer regiment in the Spanish-American War?

90) Capital city of Argentina?

91) Louis XIV's definition of the state?

92) What German military leader was known as the Desert Fox for his achievements in northern Africa?

93) What is the name of the Israeli desert that meets the tip of the Gulf of Aqaba?

94) By 1400 the Black Death had reduced the previous century's population of Europe by:
   a. 25% or more
   b. 50
   c. 75
   d. 10

# . . . Answers

86. a

87. The International Brigade

88. Pennsylvania

89. The Rough Riders

90. Buenos Aires

91. L'etat, c'est moi (I am the state)

92. Rommel

93. Negev

94. c

95) What was the major pass between Pakistan and Afghanistan that saw renowned action in the 19th century Afghan wars with the British?

96) During 1958–61 the United Arab Republic was composed of what two countries?

97) Which one of these 5th century barbarian invaders remained nomads and never formed a fixed kingdom?
    a. Visigoths
    b. Vandals
    c. Ostrogoths
    d. Huns
    e. Franks

98) Chain of islands off the southern tip of Florida?

99) Which courtier fell from Elizabeth I's favor when he reportedly seduced one of her maids of honor?

100) Where is the world's driest spot?

101) Rosa Luxemburg was assassinated in Berlin as a
    a. Marxist agitator
    b. American spy
    c. mistress of the Kaiser
    d. temperance movement leader

102) State capital of Tennessee?

# ... *Answers*

95. Khyber Pass

96. Egypt and Syria

97. d

98. Florida Keys

99. Sir Walter Raleigh

100. Atacama Desert, Chile

101. a

102. Nashville

103) In what year did the first Jews arrive in New Amsterdam?

    a. 1632

    b. 1654

    c. 1699

    d. 1702

104) Capital city of Switzerland?

105) Marie Antoinette's mother?

106) Date of D-Day, the Allied landing in Normandy?

107) The Beqaa Valley in Lebanon is drained by what river?

108) Angkor Wat, the ritual center of the kings of Cambodia, was built in what century?

    a. 4th

    b. 6th

    c. 9th

    d. 12th

109) The coastal cities the Chinese were forced to cede to foreigners after the Opium War were known as what?

110) On which Hawaiian island is Pearl Harbor?

111) How many sons did Mohammed have?

112) What Cuban bay has a U.S. Navy base?

# . . . Answers

103. b

104. Bern

105. Maria Theresa of Austria and Hungary

106. June 6, 1944

107. Litani

108. d

109. Treaty ports

110. Oahu

111. None, but at least six daughters

112. Guantanamo Bay

113) Who was the 15th century fire-and-brimstone monk who gained control of Florence but ended burnt at the stake?

114) Where is the geographic center of North America?

115) Which Indian leader is known for his use of passive resistance against the British?

116) What state is known as the Mountain State?

117) "Give me liberty or give me death" — who said this, where and when?

118) Capital city of Saudi Arabia?

119) Why were Africans brought as slaves to the West Indies in the 1700s and 1800s?

120) What Hungarian cardinal was first a state prisoner and then a refugee in the U.S. embassy 1956–1971?

121) The Republic of the Philippines consists of about:
    a. 7100 islands
    b. 9300
    c. 11,400

122) The 9th century court of Charles the Bald was located in what city?

123) In 1905 Japan destroyed what country's navy?

# . . . Answers

113. Savonarola

114. Six miles west of Balta, Pierce County, North Dakota

115. Gandhi

116. West Virginia

117. Patrick Henry, at the Virginia Convention, March 23, 1775

118. Riyadh

119. To work on sugarcane plantations

120. Mindszenty

121. a

122. Paris

123. Russia's

124) Which one of the Great Lakes is entirely within U.S. territory?

125) Who ruled Britain from 5 to 40 A.D. and became the subject of a Shakespeare play?

126) What large river flows into the Gulf of California?

127) What 1929 treaties created the independent state of Vatican City in Rome?

128) Islands off Galway Bay?

129) What kind of people took part in Shays' Rebellion in Massachusetts in 1787?

130) What other European nation ceded Bombay to Britain in 1661?

131) UN secretary-general U Thant was from what country?

132) The holy city of Mecca is in what country?

133) What English king began the construction of Westminster Abbey?

134) What other monument no less famous than his tower was engineered by Gustave Eiffel?

135) The state of Tanzania was formed in 1964 from what two colonies?

# . . . *Answers*

124. Lake Michigan

125. Cymbeline

126. Colorado River

127. Lateran Treaties

128. Aran Islands

129. Debt-ridden farmers

130. Portugal

131. Burma

132. Saudi Arabia

133. Edward the Confessor

134. The Statue of Liberty

135. Tanganyika and Zanzibar

136) Attila was king of what 5th century nomadic people?

137) Correct or incorrect?
   Pizarro: El Salvador
   Alvarado: Peru

138) Who fought at Dien Bien Phu?

139) How many republics are in the Soviet Union?

140) Last Islamic kingdom in Spain?

141) Who introduced Christianity into Japan during 1549–52?

142) From where in Europe were 350,000 British and French troops evacuated in May 1940?

143) Twins who founded Rome?

144) Ethnic region of Spain of which Barcelona is the capital?

145) Which leader of the French Revolution was known as the "archangel of the revolution" because of his handsomeness and incorruptibility?

146) What political party nominated Martin Van Buren for the 1848 presidential elections?

147) Highest point in Alaska?

# . . . Answers

136. The Huns

137. Incorrect, other way around

138. The Vietminh and French

139. Fifteen

140. Granada

141. St. Francis Xavier

142. Dunkirk

143. Romulus and Remus

144. Catalonia

145. Saint-Just

146. The Free-Soil Party

147. Mount McKinley

148) The British fleet in the 1890s was equal to the combined fleets of the two next biggest naval powers, which were?

149) Where is the burial place of Thomas Paine?

150) State capital of Maine?

151) What is the name given to ancient American Indians who left distinct traces in the Ohio Valley?

152) What Tennesseean became president of Nicaragua and tried to join that country to the Confederate states?

153) What is the coldest ever place in North America?

154) If Plymouth was not the first New England settlement, what was?

155) How close a cousin was Franklin D. to Theodore Roosevelt?

156) The island of Hispaniola is divided into what two countries?

157) Afghanistan is slightly smaller than:
    a. Texas
    b. New Jersey
    c. Michigan

# . . . Answers

148. France and Russia

149. Unknown; after he died in the United States, his body was denied burial in consecrated ground and then lost when returned to England for burial

150. Augusta

151. Mound Builders

152. William Walker

153. Snag, Yukon, Canada, with minus 81 degrees

154. The 1607 Kennebec River settlement in Maine, which was unsuccessful

155. Fifth cousin

156. Haiti and the Dominican Republic

157. a

158) What was the name of the stone with various scripts, found in Egypt in 1799, that enabled hyieroglyphics to be understood for the first time?

159) Why was the Magna Carta not signed by the English king?

160) Capital city of Cambodia?

161) What is the name of the strait between the Soviet Union and Alaska?

162) What was an 1819 massacre of unarmed civilians by soldiers at St. Peter's Field, Manchester, England, called to contrast it mockingly with Waterloo?

163) Who was the Republican Party's first president?

164) The earliest authenticated king of ancient Rome was not a Roman at all, but what?

165) Atlantic islands due west of Lisbon?

166) Who did Napoleon defeat at Austerlitz?

167) What was the leaders' motto in the French Revolution?

168) Highest point in Nevada?

# . . . Answers

158. Rosetta stone

159. Because he sealed it with his signet ring and probably did not know how to write

160. Phnum Penh

161. Bering Strait

162. Peterloo Massacre

163. Abraham Lincoln

164. An Etruscan, Tarquinius Priscus

165. Azores

166. The Russians

167. Liberty, Equality and Fraternity

168. Boundary Peak

169) What was the name of Germany's World War I plan that involved attacking France through Belgium and then swinging back to attack Russia?

170) First name of the founder of Harvard College?

171) What state is known as the Magnolia State?

172) Who was the first Hanoverian king of England?

173) The North American continent was spanned by rail from coast to coast when the Central Pacific and Union Pacific were linked by a rail held with a golden spike at what place?

174) What two ancient Roman cities can be seen dug out of volcanic ash?

175) What trade did the 15th and 16th century Portuguese hope to control between Asia and Europe?

176) What incident of 1933 did the German Nazis use to justify emergency decrees, imprisoning opponents and vesting more power in themselves?

177) Bangladesh is mostly the alluvial plain of what two great rivers?

178) The kings of ancient Egypt are usually classified according to what?

# . . . Answers

169. Schlieffen Plan

170. John

171. Mississippi

172. George I

173. Promontory, Utah

174. Pompeii and Herculaneum

175. The spice trade

176. The burning of the Reichstag

177. The Ganges and Brahmaputra

178. Dynasty

179) What English king was defeated by the Normans at the Battle of Hastings?

180) What Caribbean island is northeast of Trinidad?

181) What is the name of the big swamp in southeastern Georgia from which the Suwannee River flows?

182) Who liberated 19th century Sicily and Naples?

183) Year of Senator Joseph McCarthy's televised hearings on communist influence in the U.S. Army?

184) In ancient Rome, could the Vestal Virgins decide to quit?

185) What lake in Scotland is said to hold one or more monsters?

186) Derogatory term for Napoleon concerning stature and military rank?

187) Who was U.S. president between James K. Polk and Millard Fillmore?

188) What is the highest mountain in the Western Hemisphere?

189) Lenin's real last name?

190) Where in Philadelphia did the First Continental Congress meet?

# ... *Answers*

179.  Harold II

180.  Tobago

181.  Okefenokee

182.  Garibaldi

183.  1954

184.  No, but they were allowed to retire after 30 years

185.  Loch Ness

186.  The Little Corporal

187.  Zachary Taylor

188.  Aconcagua, in the Argentine-Chile Andes

189.  Ulyanov

190.  Carpenters Hall

191) What state is known as the Granite State?

192) The Erie Canal connects what two cities on what two waterways?

193) Which side in the American Civil War had most soldiers killed?

194) On what river is Strasbourg built?

195) Where did Luther display his "Ninety-Five Theses"?

196) Name of French fascist party?

197) Ghana is slightly smaller than:
    a. Vermont
    b. California
    c. Oregon

198) The ancient Phoenicians were famed as what?

199) In the tomb effigy of a knight, what arrangement of his body indicates he fought in the Crusades?

200) State capital of Arkansas?

201) Pre-European residents of New Zealand?

202) In which state are the Berkshire Mountains?

# . . . Answers

191. New Hampshire

192. Buffalo on Lake Erie and Albany on the Hudson River

193. The Union, with 360,000; the Confederates lost 260,000

194. Rhine

195. On a church door in Wittenberg

196. Croix de Feu (Fiery Cross)

197. c

198. Explorer-traders

199. Legs crossed

200. Little Rock

201. Maoris

202. Massachusetts

203) Name of gunman who shot George Wallace in 1972?

204) Name the six most highly populated cities in the United States.

205) What general was Julius Caesar's great enemy in Rome before he seized power?

206) What is the famous port across the Strait of Gibraltar from Spain?

207) Who did Napoleon impose on Spain as its ruler?

208) What two Roman generals, one a plebeian and the other an aristocrat, reduced Rome to civil war with their bloody rivalry?

209) Where is Mammoth Cave?

210) With German inflation, one gold mark worth 46 paper marks in December 1921 was worth how many paper marks in December 1922?
   a. 1757
   b. 1302
   c. 1119
   d. 144

211) Zimbabwe is nearly as large as:
   a. California
   b. Texas
   c. Alaska

# . . . Answers

203. Arthur H. Bremer

204. New York, Chicago, Los Angeles, Philadelphia, Houston and Detroit

205. Pompey

206. Tangier

207. His brother Joseph Bonaparte

208. Marius and Sulla

209. Kentucky

210. a

211. a

212) When called upon to surrender, what American revolutionary replied, "Sir, I have not yet begun to fight"?

213) The Great Smoky Mountains are in which two states?

214) The population of New York City in 1911 was almost:
    a. 1 million
    b. 2 million
    c. 3 million
    d. 4 million

215) In what American city is the John Hancock Tower?

216) What two countries fought the Hundred Years' War?

217) How many big islands is New Zealand composed of?

218) What was the equivalent of the United Nations between the two world wars?

219) Did the Celts ever sack Rome?

220) Iceland is the same size as:
    a. New Jersey
    b. Virginia
    c. Montana

# . . . Answers

212. John Paul Jones

213. Tennessee and North Carolina

214. d

215. Chicago

216. France and England

217. Two

218. The League of Nations

219. Yes, in 390 B.C.

220. b

221) The system of ideals of medieval knights?

222) What state is known as the Hoosier State?

223) The British bought Singapore in 1819 from what person?

224) What are the evergreen forests of southern New Jersey called?

225) In what year was De Gaulle elected president of France?

226) Did ancient Roman carriages that operated as taxis have meters?

227) What city is near the mouth of the Amazon?

228) Where was the Helvetic Republic (1798–1803)?

229) Which Spanish king first tried to marry Elizabeth I of England and later sent a fleet against her?

230) Between what two states does the Mason-Dixon Line run?

231) By 1932, in the depths of the Depression, about how many people were out of work in the United States?
    a. 6 million
    b. 12 million
    c. 18 million
    d. 24 million

# . . . Answers

221. Chivalry

222. Indiana

223. The Sultan of Johore

224. The Pine Barrens

225. 1958

226. Yes; on each complete turn of the dial hand, a pebble dropped into a box and the passenger was charged according to the number of pebbles

227. Belém

228. Switzerland

229. Philip II

230. Pennsylvania and Maryland

231. b

232) State capital of Pennsylvania?

233) Who was the first Roman Catholic to run for the U.S. presidency?

234) Capital city of Uruguay?

235) Louis XIV's magnificent palace 12 miles west of Paris?

236) Which of Germany's most brilliant generals was forced to take poison after being involved in the 1944 bomb attempt on Hitler's life?

237) Kenya is slightly smaller than:
    a. Alaska
    b. Texas
    c. North Dakota

238) Where was the Battle of Lepanto fought?
    a. in the Alps
    b. outside the walls of Constantinople
    c. in northern Africa
    d. at sea

239) What British explorer found the source of the Nile?

240) Who was the leader of the Chinese Nationalist army who drove the communists from Shanghai in 1927?

# . . . Answers

232. Harrisburg

233. Gov. Alfred E. Smith of New York in 1928

234. Montevideo

235. Versailles

236. Rommel

237. b

238. d

239. John Speke

240. Chiang Kai-shek

241) When did the Roman Empire split in two, with eastern and western emperors?

    a. 247 A.D.                   c. 432 A.D.

    b. 364 A.D.                   d. 517 A.D.

242) Seafarers respect what two North Carolina capes?

243) Who was the first English circumnavigator of the globe?

244) Where is the world's coldest spot?

245) How long was Mao's 1930s Long March?

246) What state is known as the Beehive State?

247) What is the name of the Dane, employed by the Russians, who claimed Alaska?

248) Capital city of Hungary?

249) What was the Hapsburg lip?

250) Who was the commander of the Soviet forces that stormed Berlin?

251) The Kingdom of Lesotho is completely surrounded by what country?

# . . . *Answers*

241. b

242. Cape Fear and Cape Hatteras

243. Sir Francis Drake

244. Vostok, Antarctica

245. 5000 miles

246. Utah

247. Bering

248. Budapest

249. A protuding lower lip, characteristic of 18 generations of Hapsburgs

250. Zhukov

251. South Africa

252) Timbuktu in the 14th century was an important center in which of these African empires?
  a. Benin
  b. Mali
  c. Hausa
  d. Ghana

253) In China's Taiping Rebellion (1850–64), how many people were killed?
  a. 800,000
  b. 1,400,000
  c. 2,500,000
  d. 25,000,000

254) What date was Pearl Harbor bombed?

255) In which century was Mohammed born?

256) Name of the strait between Cuba and Haiti?

257) Who did Spartacus lead in his insurrection?

258) Which has the longer coastline, Alabama or Mississippi?

259) What is the name of the 1919 occurrence in which British troops killed over 300 unarmed Indian protestors?

260) State capital of West Virginia?

# . . . Answers

252. b

253. d

254. Dec. 7, 1941

255. 6th century

256. Windward Passage

257. Roman slaves

258. Alabama, with 53 miles against 44

259. Amritsar massacre

260. Charleston

261) What was the name of the black man killed by British troops in the Boston massacre?

262) Capital city of Jordan?

263) In the late 1700s, which nation transported twice as many slaves as any other to the New World?

264) Who was the liberal Czechoslovak leader overthrown by the Soviet-led 1968 invasion?

265) What mountains run along the southern border of Poland?

266) Name of Mohammed's flight from Mecca to Medina?

267) The "mad monk" who influenced the Czarina?

268) What Canadian city is directly south of what American city?

269) What does the Roman emperor's name Caligula mean?

270) What large river flows through Leningrad?

271) What is the name of the 1935 Nazi laws that deprived German Jews of citizenship and other rights?

272) Islands off the Mediterranean coast of Spain?

# . . . *Answers*

261. Crispus Attucks

262. Amman

263. The British

264. Dubcek

265. Carpathians

266. Hegira

267. Rasputin

268. Windsor is south of Detroit

269. "Little Boots"

270. Neva

271. Nuremberg Laws

272. Balearic Islands

273) Wayne, the American general in command of the Ohio-Indiana area, was commonly known by what name?

274) Emperor Meiji moved his court to Edo, which he renamed what?

275) What part of Nigeria unsuccessfully tried to secede in a civil war?

276) Which two Dutch colonies became part of the Union of South Africa in 1910?

277) What did Macbeth become king of after murdering Duncan?

278) What 19th century French officer was unjustly convicted of spying for Germany, with anti-Semitic and ultraconservative groups trying to prevent his retrial?

279) Who reached the South Pole first, and when?

280) Odoacer was chieftain of what barbarian people?

281) What was Martin Frobisher searching for during 1576–77?

282) What was the name of South Vietnam's prime minister whose authoritarian ways led to his assassination in 1963?

# . . . Answers

273. Mad Anthony

274. Tokyo

275. Biafra

276. Transvaal and Orange Free State

277. Scotland

278. Captain Alfred Dreyfus

279. Amundsen, in 1911

280. Ostrogoths

281. The Northwest Passage

282. Ngo Dinh Diem

283) What chain of mountains divide the Soviet Union into European and Asiatic sections?

284) What representative body of all classes did Edward I of England call in 1295?

285) What is the collective name of the individuals blamed after Mao's death for China's excesses?

286) As infants, the twins who founded Rome were said to have been suckled by?

287) Texas west of the Pecos and north of the Rio Grande is what country?

288) Name of French historical period during the reign of Napoleon III?

289) What French revolutionary said, "We must dare and dare, and dare again—and France is saved"?

290) Highest point in Arizona?

291) Whose assassination at Sarajevo triggered World War I?

292) What song was used by British troops to poke fun at American troops during the Revolution, then adopted by Americans as their own?

293) What state is known as the Old Line State?

# . . . Answers

283. Urals

284. His "Model Parliament"

285. The Gang of Four

286. A she-wolf

287. Big Bend country

288. Second Empire

289. Danton

290. Humphreys Peak

291. Archduke Franz Ferdinand and his wife

292. Yankee Doodle

293. Maryland

294) Custer died in what battle?

295) Who was the first American when offered the presidential nomination to reply, "I will not accept if nominated, and will not serve if elected"?

296) What is the world's wettest place?

297) Where did Captain Bligh of the *Bounty* face a second mutiny?

298) What did Franklin D. Roosevelt call his frequent radio broadcasts while president?

299) What country did Bernardo O'Higgins rule during 1818–1823?

300) Albania is slightly larger than:
    a. Rhode Island
    b. Arizona
    c. Maryland

301) What four initials represented the power of the Roman senate and people throughout the empire?

302) The Arab advance into northern Europe was stopped at Poitiers by the Franks in 732 under whose leadership?

303) Capital city of Malaysia?

304) Which four U.S. states meet at a single point?

# ... Answers

294. The Little Big Horn

295. William Tecumseh Sherman, in 1884

296. Mount Maialeale, Hawaii, with an annual rainfall of 460 inches

297. In an Australian penal colony

298. Fireside chats

299. Chile

300. c

301. S.P.Q.R. (Senatus Populusque Romanus)

302. Charles Martel

303. Kuala Lumpur

304. Utah, Colorado, New Mexico and Arizona

305) In what single year of the 19th century did a rebellion occur in almost every European country?

306) In 1867 the Grange was organized in America to protect who?

307) The ruling class of ancient Rome was known as what?

308) Portuguese islands off Morocco?

309) Who did Napolean defeat at Jena and Auerstadt?

310) Who was the minister of propaganda in Nazi Germany?

311) Highest point in New Mexico?

312) How many colonies did Germany get to keep after World War I?

313) In 1763 France lost all its possessions in Canada except for one small island group, which it still holds today and which is named?

314) State capital of Mississippi?

315) Who wandered through the streets of Baltimore during the 1856 presidential election intent on keeping Irish and German immigrants from voting?

# . . . *Answers*

305. 1848

306. Farmers

307. Patricians

308. Madeira

309. The Prussians

310. Goebbels

311. Wheeler Peak

312. None

313. St. Pierre et Miquelon

314. Jackson

315. The Know-Nothings

316) What French leader sold Louisiana to the United States?

317) How long is the Great Wall of China?

318) Amerigo Vespucci, from what part of Italy, went where and on whose behalf?

319) What was the name given the 6500 German airforce troops that used the Spanish Civil War as a training exercise?

320) Lake Titicaca is between what two countries?

321) Which is nearest the Mediterranean, ancient Upper or Lower Egypt?

322) Where did the Normans who attacked England come from?

323) What Caribbean island is west of Curaçao?

324) Which Hawaiian city is sometimes threatened by lava from Mauna Kea volcano?

325) Who was the man responsible for uniting 19th century Italy?

326) In what year previous to 1983 did U.S. Marines land in Lebanon to protect the government?

# . . . Answers

316. Napoleon

317. 1500 miles

318. From Florence, he went to the north coast of South America and Brazil on behalf of the Spanish

319. The Condor Legion

320. Peru and Bolivia

321. Lower Egypt

322. The north of France, Normandy

323. Aruba

324. Hilo

325. Cavour

326. 1958

# QUESTIONS

327) Which of these were in charge of early Rome's finances?
   a. aediles
   b. lictors
   c. censors
   d. quaestors

328) What is the name of the gulf between Sweden and Finland?

329) Napoleon's first wife's name?

330) Who was U.S. president between Franklin Pierce and Abraham Lincoln?

331) What is the highest mountain in North America?

332) Lenin gave in to the peasants in 1921, allowing them to market their produce, in what policy?

333) Which colony did not attend the First Continental Congress in Philadelphia?

334) State capital of New Hampshire?

335) Where was the site of the world's first successful oil well?

336) Where and when was the Ku Klux Klan founded?

337) On what river is Bordeaux built?

# . . . Answers

327. d

328. Gulf of Bothnia

329. Joséphine Beauharnais

330. James Buchanan

331. Mount McKinley in Alaska

332. The New Economic Policy

333. Georgia

334. Concord

335. Titusville, Pa.

336. In Pulaski, Tenn., in 1866

337. Garonne

338) Who was slaughtered in the Massacre of St. Bartholomew's Day?

339) What was the name of the Austrian chancellor murdered in 1934 on Hitler's orders?

340) Grenada is twice the size of:
   a. Washington, D.C.
   b. Delaware
   c. Rhode Island

341) Who was the first king of the ancient Hebrews?

342) When thousands of children set out from medieval France and Germany, later to be sold into slavery or die of hunger or disease, what was their purpose?

343) Pikes Peak is in which state?

344) European colonizers of Indonesian islands?

345) Sault Ste. Marie is between which two of the Great Lakes?

346) What organization's offices were broken into at Watergate in 1972?

347) What is the major river of Venezuela?

348) Who succeeded Julius Caesar as ruler of Rome?

349) In what country is the Nubian Desert?

# . . . *Answers*

338.  French Protestants (Huguenots)

339.  Dollfuss

340.  a

341.  Saul

342.  The Children's Crusade to the Holy Land

343.  Colorado

344.  The Dutch

345.  Superior and Huron

346.  The Democratic National Committee

347.  Orinoco

348.  Octavian, who became known as Caesar Augustus

349.  Sudan

350) Who is known as "the Liberator" throughout South America?

351) Nickname of Mary Tudor, who persecuted Protestants when she was queen of England?

352) Where is Wyandotte Cave?

353) Franklin D. Roosevelt defeated who in the 1932 presidential election?

354) Correct or incorrect?
   Northern Rhodesia: Zimbabwe
   Southern Rhodesia: Zambia

355) What is the name of John Paul Jones' famous ship during the American Revolution?

356) In which state is the Wright Brothers National Monument at Kitty Hawk?

357) Last czar of Russia?

358) What was the date of an armed invasion of New Jersey by Martians?

359) What was Europe's population in 1700?
   a. 104 million
   b. 115 million
   c. 135 million
   d. 142 million

# . . . *Answers*

350. Simón Bolívar

351. Bloody Mary

352. Indiana

353. Herbert Hoover

354. Incorrect, other way around

355. *Bon Homme Richard*

356. North Carolina

357. Nicholas II

358. Oct. 30, 1938, according to Orson Welles' radio broadcast

359. b

360) Capital city of Venezuela?

361) Which country had by far the highest casualties of World War II?

362) Where did the Etruscans live?

363) Indonesia is composed of how many islands?
   a. 700
   b. 1150
   c. 13,500

364) At the time of Marco Polo's departure for Asia in 1271, what was the busiest port in the world?

365) What state is known as the Hawkeye State?

366) From what other European nation did the British buy the African Gold Coast settlements in 1850?

367) What is the name of a group of long, narrow, almost parallel lakes in west central New York State?

368) Who was the clergyman leader of the Greek Cypriots and first president of independent Cyprus?

369) Approximately when was the Great Wall of China begun?

370) What city is halfway up the Amazon?

371) Where was the Cisalpine Republic (1797–1805)?

# . . . *Answers*

360. Caracas

361. Russia

362. Northern Italy

363. c

364. Venice

365. Iowa

366. Denmark

367. The Finger Lakes

368. Archbishop Makarios

369. In the 4th and 3rd centuries B.C.

370. Manaus

371. Northern Italy

372) The Elder Pitt and the Younger Pitt both held what position in Great Britain?

373) What is the northernmost point of the United States?

374) Approximately how many Americans fought in the Spanish Civil War?
   a. 500
   b. 1550
   c. 2800
   d. 3300

375) What state is known as the Ocean State?

376) On what day in what year did Christopher Columbus sight land in the present-day Bahamas?

377) Capital city of Paraguay?

378) Which palace was a favorite of French royal families, 37 miles southeast of Paris and next to a forest?

379) Who was the commander of U.S. Navy forces in the Pacific during World War II?

380) South Korea is slightly larger than:
   a. Kansas
   b. Vermont
   c. Indiana

# . . . *Answers*

372. Prime minister

373. Point Barrow, Alaska

374. c

375. Rhode Island

376. Oct. 12, 1492

377. Asunción

378. Fontainebleau

379. Nimitz

380. c

381) Who gave Europe its first detailed account of China?

382) Mungo _____ , Scottish explorer of West Africa?

383) What is the name of the Indian who became prime minister by beating Mrs. Gandhi in the 1977 election?

384) Who was the last western Roman emperor?
   a. Julius Nepos
   b. Romulus Augustulus
   c. Leo
   d. Olybrius

385) What major California headland is west of Santa Barbara?

386) Who was Nazi ambassador to Britain before World War II, foreign minister during it and sentenced to death at Nuremberg after it?

387) Where is the world's hottest spot?

388) Who was responsible for the Rape of Nanking?

389) In which state is Bryce Canyon?

390) What American hired by the British to fight pirates became one himself and was hanged in England in 1701?

# . . . Answers

381. Marco Polo

382. Park

383. Morarji R. Desai

384. b

385. Point Conception

386. Ribbentrop

387. Al'Aziziyah, Libya

388. The Japanese

389. Utah

390. Captain William Kidd

391) Capital city of Czechoslovakia?

392) With which absolute ruler did Voltaire quarrel, saying he was tired of correcting the man's French grammar?

393) On which was the atomic bomb dropped first, Hiroshima or Nagasaki?

394) The Principality of Liechtenstein is between what two countries?

395) Which built their empire first, the Mayas or the Aztecs?

396) Two of the major Chinese 19th century rebellions involved uprisings by:
    a. mandarins
    b. Muslims
    c. students
    d. military

397) The International Monetary Fund was established in 1944 at what New Hampshire meeting?

398) What was the name of the military caste of former Turks, Kurds and Circassians which ruled Egypt and the Middle East in the 12th and 13th centuries?

399) What is the name of the huge, almost landlocked sea inlet from the Gulf of Venezuela?

# . . . Answers

391. Prague

392. Frederick the Great of Prussia

393. Hiroshima

394. Switzerland and Austria

395. The Mayas

396. b

397. The Bretton Woods Conference

398. The Mamelukes

399. Lake Maracaibo

400) In what area of the Soviet Union was Stalin born?

401) Which has the longer coastline, Texas or Louisiana?

402) The British Commonwealth occupies what fraction of the world's land surface?

403) In which state is Harpers Ferry National Historic Park?

404) What night of the year 1775 did Paul Revere make his famous ride?

405) Capital city of Iraq?

406) Which company founded in Canada in 1670 to buy furs from the Indians is still in business there today?

407) In what year did the Hungarian uprising against Soviet occupation take place?

408) Portugal is slightly smaller than:
   a. Colorado
   b. Indiana
   c. Vermont

409) Who established a Viking colony in Greenland about 985?

410) St. Petersburg's "Bloody Sunday" was in what year?

# . . . Answers

400. Georgia

401. Lousiana, with 397 miles against 367

402. One-quarter

403. West Virginia

404. April 18

405. Baghdad

406. The Hudson's Bay Company

407. 1956

408. b

409. Eric the Red

410. 1905

411) Lake St. Clair is a smaller lake on a river connecting which two of the Great Lakes?

412) What is the name of the British queen who led the revolt against the occupying Romans at Londinium?

413) What American Indian nation set out on the "Trail of Tears" in 1838?

414) Who was head of the Vichy government?

415) Island nation south of Sicily?

416) Where did the Whiskey Rebellion of 1794 occur?

417) What American naval officer broke Japan's isolationist policy in 1853?

418) Which copper-rich province of what was once the Belgian Congo tried to secede and involved UN troops in a peace-keeping role?

419) What were the two British colonies that became part of the Union of South Africa in 1910?

420) Early name for the Tower of London?

421) How long did the Paris Commune hold out for against the rest of France?

422) Who was West Germany's first chancellor, the man who led the country in its postwar recovery?

# . . . *Answers*

411. Huron and Erie

412. Boadicea

413. Cherokee

414. Pétain

415. Malta

416. Pennsylvania

417. Commodore Perry

418. Katanga

419. The Cape Colony and Natal

420. The White Tower

421. Two months, March-May 1871

422. Adenauer

423) Clovis I, king of the Franks, ended Roman rule in Gaul and founded what dynasty?

424) Who is the best known villain of the 1605 Gunpowder Plot?

425) First prime minister of Israel?

426) What is Ireland's longest river?

427) The kingdom of Benin in Nigeria had established trade with what European nation by 1490?

428) German battleship scuttled off Montevideo?

429) How was a new colony made official in Rome's early days?
   a. statues of Roman gods were erected in the town square
   b. its founder guided a plow around its boundaries
   c. a special seal was carved in stone

430) Mountain in northern Wales, its name assumed by a photographer earl?

431) What former royal palace has served as a granary, prison, arsenal, leper colony, mint, telegraph station and whorehouse before becoming an art museum?

432) What was the name of the most fanatical of the leaders of the French Revolution, the man who dominated the Committee of Public Safety?

# . . . Answers

423. Merovingian

424. Guy Fawkes

425. Ben-Gurion

426. Shannon

427. Portugal

428. *Graf Spee*

429. b

430. Snowdon

431. The Louvre

432. Robespierre

433) Highest point in California?

434) What was the Sarajevo assassin's name?

435) How many people were executed at the Salem witch hunt?

436) State capital of Maryland?

437) Who was the only man besides George Washington to run unopposed for the U.S. presidency?

438) What Mexican general attacked the Alamo?

439) On average, how many miles to the moon?

440) The Marquise de Maintenon was first governess to the children of, then mistress of, finally second wife of which French king?

441) How many major Nazi leaders went on trial after the war at Nuremberg?

442) What country was founded by freed American slaves returned to Africa?

443) What are the fertile treeless plains of Argentina called?

444) What were the first two kinds of animals domesticated by humankind?

# . . . *Answers*

433. Mount Whitney

434. Gavrilo Princip

435. 19 were hanged and one was pressed to death

436. Annapolis

437. James Monroe in 1820

438. Santa Anna

439. An average of 238,857 miles

440. Louis XIV

441. 22

442. Liberia

443. Pampas

444. Sheep and goats

445) On Christmas Day, 800, who did the pope crown in St. Peter's as Holy Roman Emperor?

446) Capital city of Australia?

447) What separate Indian reservation is entirely surrounded by the Navajo reservation?

448) Why was Paris given broad boulevards after 1848?

449) What was the name of the 1870s Irish terrorist group in Pennsylvania mining areas?

450) What were the two most powerful positions in the early Roman republic?

451) Spanish islands off Morocco?

452) Admiral Nelson's first name?

453) What did the Chinese emperor present to the English soldier Gordon in recognition of his services in quelling rebellions?

454) Highest point in Oregon?

455) What was the name of the peace agreement imposed on Germany after World War I?

456) Who founded the doomed colony on Roanoke Island off North Carolina?

# . . . *Answers*

445.  Charlemagne

446.  Canberra

447.  Hopi reservation

448.  To facilitate cavalry charges against city mobs

449.  The Molly Maguires

450.  The two elected consuls

451.  Canary Islands

452.  Horatio

453.  The yellow jacket and peacock's feather of a mandarin of the first class

454.  Mount Hood

455.  Treaty of Versailles

456.  Sir Walter Raleigh

457) What state is known as the Show Me State?

458) Who did underdog Harry S. Truman defeat in the 1948 presidential election?

459) What was the deal called in which a strip of land was purchased from Mexico in 1953 to provide access for a transcontinental railroad?

460) What is the name of the Roman wall across northern Britain?

461) Aztec ruler imprisoned by Cortés?

462) What was Mussolini before he became a political leader?

463) Bulgaria is slightly larger than:
   a. Tennessee
   b. Wyoming
   c. Connecticut

464) Ancient Indian civilization, including the city of Mohenjo-daro, took place along the valley of what river?

465) Spanish Muslims were known as?

466) What state is known as the Heart of Dixie?

467) What river forms the border between Indiana and Kentucky?

# . . . Answers

457. Missouri

458. Thomas E. Dewey

459. The Gadsden Purchase

460. Hadrian's Wall

461. Montezuma

462. A schoolteacher

463. a

464. Indus

465. Moors

466. Alabama

467. Ohio River

468) Who won the Franco-Prussian War?

469) Alaska and Hawaii were admitted as states in what year?

470) What was the title of the two men in charge of early Rome's public morals?

471) What very large lake is near Leningrad?

472) Napoleon's second wife's name?

473) Who was U.S. president between James A. Garfield and Grover Cleveland?

474) What is the largest lake in the world?

475) Who seized the Winter Palace as they overthrew the government?

476) What was the first clash between American colonists and British soldiers?

477) What state is known as the Garden State?

478) Capital and most important city of the Confederacy?

479) Approximately how many immigrants entered the United States between the Civil War and World War I?
    a. 10 million        c. 30 million
    b. 20 million        d. 40 million

# . . . *Answers*

468. Prussia

469. 1959

470. Censors

471. Lake Ladoga

472. Marie Louise, Archduchess of Austria

473. Chester A. Arthur

474. Caspian Sea

475. Lenin's Bolsheviks

476. The Boston Massacre in 1770

477. New Jersey

478. Richmond, Va.

479. b

480) On what river is Florence built?

481) In the English civil wars, the Royalists and Parliamentarians were popularly known by what names?

482) What was the term used by Hitler to describe Germany's need for more territory to the east?

483) Honduras is slightly larger than:
   a. Utah
   b. Tennessee
   c. Massachusetts

484) How many northern tribes of ancient Israel were scattered and lost?

485) The 11th century saw the founding of the Carthusians and Cistercians, which were what?

486) What state is known as the Nutmeg State?

487) In 1900 which European nation had colonies more than three times the area of those of its nearest rival?

488) Lake of the Woods forms part of the border between Canada and what American state?

489) Name of Watergate case judge?

490) Columbus first set foot on the South American continent on the peninsula of Paria, which is in what present-day country?

# . . . Answers

480. Arno

481. Cavaliers and Roundheads

482. Lebensraum (living space)

483. b

484. Ten

485. Orders of monks

486. Connecticut

487. Great Britain

488. Minnesota

489. John Sirica

490. Venezuela

491) What language did Jesus speak?

492) Where is the Nullarbor Plain?

493) Whose "Army of the Andes" crossed the mountains in a surprise attack to liberate Chile?

494) What was the name of the Austrian emperor's brother who was persuaded to become emperor of Mexico?

495) What is the lowest point in North America?

496) How many times was Franklin D. Roosevelt elected president?

497) Country of birth of John Paul Jones?

498) What state is known as the Flickertail State?

499) Abraham's Lincoln's birthplace?

500) Who was the only American president to remain unmarried?

501) In the 1500s, what European country was twice as wealthy as the next richest country and ten times wealthier than most?

502) Capital city of Nicaragua?

# . . . Answers

491. Aramaic

492. Australia

493. José de San Martín's

494. Maximilian

495. Death Valley, Calif.

496. Four

497. Scotland

498. North Dakota

499. Hodgenville, Ky.

500. James Buchanan

501. Spain

502. Managua

503) Compared with World War I *military* casualties, World War II *military* casualties were:
    a. much less             c. much greater
    b. almost the same

504) What people developed the first large civilization in the Western Hemisphere?

505) What mountains run down through the center of the Italian peninsula?

506) All 14th century peasant rebellions in Europe had a similar cause, which was:
    a. the church demanded exorbitant contributions
    b. landowners tried to keep down wages during a labor shortage
    c. lack of organized help for plague victims
    d. demand for a share in government

507) State capital of Iowa?

508) What was the name of the cool British summer capital in the Indian foothills?

509) What large river runs more or less from north to south through the Dakotas?

510) In what year was the Berlin Wall erected?

511) During which of these spans did Confucius live?
    a. 14-86 A.D.           c. 551-479 B.C.
    b. 328-256 B.C.        d. 764-692 B.C.

## . . . Answers

503. b; civilian casualties more than doubled the World War II toll

504. The Olmecs, about 1200 B.C.

505. Appenine Mountains

506. b

507. Des Moines

508. Simla

509. Missouri

510. 1961

511. c

512) What is the seafaring name for the southern tip of South America?

513) Where was the Ligurian Republic (1797-1805)?

514) Who was commander-in-chief of the American revolutionary forces for their defeat in the Battle of Long Island?

515) What is the easternmost point of the United States?

516) Alexander II of Russia was assassinated in 1881 by:

     a. his own imperial guard
     b. anarchists
     c. religious fanatics
     d. Bolsheviks

517) What state is known as the Palmetto State?

518) Who razed St. Augustine, Fla., in 1586?

519) Capital city of Chile?

520) Peter the Great and Catherine the Great of Russia belonged to what dynasty?

521) Who was the winning general at El Alamein?

522) Where is the Republic of Kiribati?

# . . . *Answers*

512. Cape Horn

513. Genoa

514. Israel Putnam

515. West Quoddy Head, Maine

516. b

517. South Carolina

518. Sir Francis Drake

519. Santiago

520. Romanov

521. Montgomery

522. Micronesian islands in the Pacific

523) When Marco Polo reached Peking, who was ruler there?

524) Stanley and Livingstone — which found the other?

525) In what year was the Panama Canal opened?

526) Constantinople, capital of the Byzantine empire, finally fell in 1453 to:
   a. the Ottoman Turks    c. Germanic invaders
   b. the Seljuks          d. the Slavs

527) What is the major cape of the northernmost part of California?

528) What is the name of the pass in the Pyrenees in which Charlemagne's rearguard was ambushed and defeated?

529) Where is the world's northermost town?

530) Aboard which American ship was Japan's World War II surrender signed?

531) State capital of Vermont?

532) With which Indians did William Penn sign a treaty?

533) Capital city of Rumania?

534) What two disasters hit London in 1665 and 1666?

# ... *Answers*

523. Kublai Kham

524. Stanley found Livingstone

525. 1914

526. a

527. Cape Mendocino

528. Roncesvalles

529. Ny Alesund, Spitsbergen, Norway

530. USS *Missouri*

531. Montpelier

532. The Delawares

533. Bucharest

534. 1665, the great plague; 1666, the great fire

535) What was the name of the Soviet chief of secret police who was tried and executed after Stalin's death?

536) The Grand Duchy of Luxembourg is between what three countries?

537) Which was the most organized and powerful pre-Columbian civilization in the Western Hemisphere?

538) The 1900 uprising against foreigners in China by a secret society of the "righteous and harmonious fist" became known as what?

539) The United States, Britain and the Soviet Union made plans for an international organization at what 1944 meeting near Washington, D.C.?

540) The title czar is a Russian version of what ancient name?

541) Which two South American countries have no access to the sea?

542) What country was Trotsky living in when he was murdered?

543) What is the highest peak in Africa?

544) What was the nickname of World War I American general Pershing?

545) What state is known as the Badger State?

# . . . Answers

535. Beria

536. Belgium, Germany and France

537. The Incas

538. The Boxer Rebellion

539. The Dumbarton Oaks Conference

540. The Roman Caesar

541. Bolivia and Paraguay

542. Mexico

543. Kilimanjaro

544. Blackjack

545. Wisconsin

546) Col. Ethan Allen and Col. Benedict Arnold captured what fort in 1775?

547) Capital city of Afghanistan?

548) Shah Jehan, Akbar and Aurungzebe all ruled where?

549) What was the name of the unsuccessful Chinese communist economic drive launched in 1958?

550) Rumania is slightly smaller than:
   a. Texas                  c. Oregon
   b. South Carolina

551) England's King Alfred the Great ruled during:
   a. 690-718                c. 732-760
   b. 714-742                d. 871-899

552) The International Red Cross was founded where and when?

553) In what year was Ghandi assassinated?

554) What are Nerva, Trajan, Hadrian, Antonius Pius and Marcus Aurelius known as?

555) What city did Peter the Great of Russia order built in Western style as "a window on Europe"?

556) What was the name of the Crimean meeting of Roosevelt, Churchill and Stalin?

# . . . *Answers*

546. Fort Ticonderoga

547. Kabul

548. India

549. The Great Leap Forward

550. c

551. d

552. At the Geneva Convention of 1864

553. 1948

554. The Five Good Emperors

555. St. Petersburg (now Leningrad)

556. Yalta Conference

557) Oil-producing island nation in the Persian Gulf?

558) Which American president in his farewell address warned of the dangers of permanent alliances with foreign powers, a big public debt, a large military establishment and the influence of special interest groups?

559) What Indian ruler built the Taj Mahal?

560) What was the name adopted by the Belgian Congo on independence?

561) What was the former residence of Scottish kings in Edinburgh?

562) What was the nickname of Frederick I, Holy Roman Emperor and King of Germany?

563) When were the Canadian provinces united as the Dominion of Canada?

564) Whose older brother was executed for the attempted assassination in 1887 of Czar Alexander III?

565) Who was the 6th century Roman monk sent to convert the English and who founded a church at Canterbury?

566) What was the name of the 1899 policy forced on China by which all nations had equal trading rights?

567) Israel became independent in what year?

# ... *Answers*

557. Bahrain

558. George Washington

559. Shah Jehan

560. Zaire

561. Holyrood

562. Barbarossa (Redbeard)

563. 1867

564. Lenin's

565. St. Augustine

566. Open Door policy

567. 1948

568) What are Britain's two longest rivers?

569) Prince Henry the Navigator ruled where?

570) What was the name of France's so-called impenetrable line of defense against the Nazis?

571) Who were the Punic Wars between?

572) In what city is the famed St. Mark's Square?

573) Which leader of the French Revolution was stabbed to death in his bath by Charlotte Corday?

574) Who was the leading agitator for Catholic emancipation in Ireland?

575) Highest point in Colorado?

576) In World War I, how many soldiers on all sides were killed?
    a. 4 million         c. 8 million
    b. 6 million         d. 10 million

577) Correct or incorrect?
    The Virginia Company of London: New England coast
    The Virginia Company of Plymouth: Virginia and Maryland

578) What state is known as the Golden State?

# . . . *Answers*

568. Severn and Thames

569. Portugal

570. The Maginot Line

571. The Romans and Carthaginians

572. Venice

573. Marat

574. Daniel O'Connell

575. Mount Elbert

576. d

577. Incorrect, other way around

578. California

579) What position did Thomas Jefferson hold in George Washington's original cabinet?

580) What was the presidential campaign slogan of successful candidate William Henry Harrison, victor over the Indians at Tippecanoe, and his running mate, John Tylor?

581) Where is 0 degrees longitude measured?

582) Which French king raced up and down the Louvre in a little carriage drawn by two mastiffs?

583) Who did John F. Kennedy defeat in 1952 for a seat in the U.S. Senate?

584) What did the 1840 Treaty of Waitangi guarantee to who?

585) Which was the first state to abolish capital punishment?

586) In what part of the world did the ancient Sumerians live?

587) Who was the Viking god of thunder and war?

588) Capital city of New Zealand?

589) In which state is the White Sands Missile Range?

# . . . *Answers*

579. Secretary of state

580. Tippecanoe and Tyler too

581. At Greenwich, east of London

582. Louis XIII

583. Henry Cabot Lodge

584. That the New Zealand Maoris would retain their land if they surrendered sovereignty to the British crown

585. Michigan, in 1847

586. The Middle East, from Syria through Mesopotamia to the Persian Gulf

587. Thor

588. Wellington

589. New Mexico

590) Why did Kaiser Wilhelm I of Prussia say that the day he was crowned German emperor was the unhappiest day in his life?

591) Year Brooklyn Bridge was opened?

592) What was the name of Hannibal of Carthage's brother?
    a. Hasdrubal        c. Superbus
    b. Scipio          d. Gaius

593) India's largest city?

594) Napoleon aimed at sealing off Europe from trading with Britain, a concept he called what?

595) What was the name of the war between British and Dutch colonists in southern Africa?

596) Highest point in Utah?

597) What was the unofficial name of the German government between World War I and Hitler's rise to power?

598) What word carved in a tree trunk was the only sign left by the vanished settlers of Roanoke Island off North Carolina?

599) State capital of Missouri?

# . . . Answers

590. He expected even more important titles

591. 1883

592. a

593. Calcutta

594. The Continental System

595. The Boer War

596. Kings Peak

597. The Weimar Republic

598. Croatoan

599. Jefferson City

600) Which amendment to the U.S. Constitution gave women the right to vote, and when was it ratified?

601) Who was president of the Confederacy?

602) On what river is Rome built?

603) Pizarro conquered who and where?

604) What was the name of Hitler's unsuccessful attempt to overthrow the Bavarian government in Munich in 1923?

605) Burma's huge river?

606) On which Mediterranean island did the ancient Minoans live?

607) Capital of Muslim Spain?
   a. Valencia
   b. Madrid
   c. Toledo
   d. Córdoba

608) State capital of Alabama?

609) Vermont has mountains of what two colors?

610) What did Giuseppe Mazzini proclaim in 1849?

611) Year of Bay of Pigs invasion?

# . . . Answers

600. The 19th Amendment, ratified in 1920

601. Jefferson Davis

602. Tiber

603. The Incas in Peru

604. The Beer-Hall Putsch

605. Irrawaddy

606. Crete

607. d

608. Montgomery

609. Green Mts., White Mts.

610. A Roman Republic

611. 1961

612) Who were the early Romans who decided the wisdom of an action from signs, often the behavior of birds?

    a. publicani           c. equites

    b. augurs            d. lictors

613) What large Soviet city is close to Finland?

614) Which Bourbon king was restored to the French throne during Napoleon's abdication?

615) Who was the U.S. president between Grover Cleveland and Theodore Roosevelt?

616) What is the largest lake in North America?

617) In what city did the Easter Rebellion occur?

618) What was the rallying cry of the early American revolutionaries?

619) State capital of New Jersey?

620) Which amendment to the U.S. Constitution created prohibition, and when was it ratified?

621) What was the name of the Confederate mounted guerrilla group with which Jesse James and Coleman Younger had ridden?

622) On what river is Seville built?

# . . . *Answers*

612. b

613. Leningrad

614. Louis XVIII

615. William McKinley

616. Lake Superior

617. Dublin

618. "Taxation without representation is tyranny"

619. Trenton

620. The 18th Amendment, ratified in 1919

621. Quantrill's Raiders

622. Guadalquivir

623) In the War of the Roses, what colors were the two emblem roses of the opposed sides?

624) What was the name of the German-speaking part of Czechoslovakia seized by Hitler?

625) El Salvador is the same size as:
    a. Florida
    b. Indiana
    c. Massachusetts

626) Of what were Cyrus and Darius the Great rulers?

627) In 1309 the papal court was forced to move from Rome to where?

628) State capital of Connecticut?

629) What was Queen Victoria's title regarding India?

630) In which state are the Mark Twain National Forests?

631) What was the name of the first Watergate special prosecutor, later fired by Nixon?

632) North Yemen and South Yemen — which is leftist?

633) Who was the first Roman to have his image on coins?

634) Where is the Murray-Darling River?

# . . . *Answers*

623. Red and white

624. The Sudetenland

625. c

626. The Persian Empire

627. Avignon, France

628. Hartford

629. Empress of India

630. Missouri

631. Archibald Cox

632. South

633. Julius Caesar

634. Australia

635) Of what country was Panama a part until the 1903 revolt?

636) Who was the greatest king of Assyria, reputed to have built the Hanging Gardens of Babylon?

637) Where is the geographic center of the 48 conterminous states?

638) In the 1929 Wall Street crash, how long did it take stock values to decline by one-third?

639) Who are being referred to in these lines?
     Here once the embattled farmers stood
     And fired the shot heard round the world.

640) State capital of North Dakota?

641) What was the name of the Washington theatre in which Lincoln was assassinated?

642) Three of the first five U.S. presidents all died on what unusual day of the year?

643) In the 17th century the Netherlands became the world's strongest economic power through:
     a. their colonies overseas
     b. their military conquests in Europe
     c. transporting the products of other countries
     d. loans to warring monarchs

644) Capital city of Costa Rica?

# . . . Answers

635. Colombia

636. Nebuchadnezzar

637. Near Lebanon, Smith County, Kansas

638. Two months

639. The revolutionaries at Concord, Mass., by Emerson

640. Bismarck

641. Ford's Theatre

642. Independence Day, July 4

643. c

644. San José

# QUESTIONS

645) What segments of British and German forces fought in the Battle of Britain?

646) Into what kind of political units was ancient Greece divided?

647) Jamaica is slightly smaller than:
   a. Connecticut
   b. Vermont
   c. Kentucky

648) In the late Middle Ages, gold coins gained wide acceptance as currency, particularly the ducat of _____ and the florin of _____.

649) What state is known as the Sunflower State?

650) What was smuggled on a large scale from India into China by the 19th century British?

651) Ohio touches on which of the Great Lakes?

652) What was the name of the last king of modern Egypt?

653) During the 13th century, who were China's conquerors from the north?

654) What is the seafaring name of the southern tip of Africa?

655) Where was the Parthenopian Republic (1799)?

# . . . *Answers*

645. The RAF and Luftwaffe

646. City-states

647. a

648. The ducat of Venice and florin of Florence

649. Kansas

650. Opium

651. Lake Erie

652. Farouk

653. The Mongols

654. Cape of Good Hope

655. Southern Italy

656) In what battle was the American Indian leader Tecumseh killed?

657) Where is the world's deepest ocean point?

658) State capital of South Carolina?

659) Who was the leader of the 1607 Jamestown, Va., settlement?

660) Capital city of Norway?

661) Who was the last British king to personally lead his troops into battle?

662) Of the original German army of 270,000 that attacked Stalingrad, how many survived long enough to surrender on Jan. 31, 1943?
    a. 0                c. 110,000
    b. 75,000         d. 140,000

663) Laos is slightly larger than:
    a. Utah            c. New Mexico
    b. West Virginia

664) Genghis Khan was the leader of what nomadic tribes?

665) In what Dutch republic in southern Africa was gold discovered in the mid-1880s?

666) Who fought in the 1932-35 Chaco War?

# . . . Answers

656. The Battle of the Thames

657. Mariana Trench in the Pacific

658. Columbia

659. Captain John Smith

660. Oslo

661. George II, in the Battle of Dettingen, Germany, in 1743

662. c

663. a

664. The Mongols

665. The Transvaal

666. Bolivia and Paraguay

667) What is the name of the sea inlet at Seattle?

668) What is the name, other than Charter Island, of the island in the Thames on which the Magna Carta was signed?

669) Where is the world's southernmost town?

670) What American general represented the Allies at Japan's World War II surrender?

671) What state is known as Old Dominion?

672) Where were the Acadian French before they were moved to Louisiana?

673) Capital city of Yugoslavia?

674) What dominated the London skyline after 1710?

675) What item of apparel was used by Khrushchev to make some points on his United Nations visit?

676) Nepal is the same size as:
   a. North Carolina
   b. Indiana
   c. Arizona

677) What was the dominant kingdom in Britain during the late 6th and early 7th centuries?

# . . . Answers

667. Puget Sound

668. Runnymede

669. Puerto Williams, Chile

670. MacArthur

671. Virginia

672. Nova Scotia

673. Belgrade

674. The dome of St. Paul's Cathedral

675. His shoe

676. a

677. Kent

678) Who was the founder of 20th century China's Kuomintang party?

679) Former name of Hawaiian Islands?

680) Henry VIII and Elizabeth I of England belonged to what dynasty?

681) Which is the only Central American country with no access to the Atlantic?

682) Who was the Dutch leader in New Amsterdam whose farm gave the Bowery its name and whose false leg reputedly was made of silver?

683) What is the deepest part of the Atlantic Ocean?

684) What World War I battle was an unsuccessful attempt to relieve Russia through Turkey?

685) State capital of Wisconsin?

686) Nathan Hale was executed as what by the British in 1776?

687) Capital city of Nepal?

688) Where was the Mogul Empire?

689) What was the name of the Chinese premier who was host to Richard Nixon on his visit to China in 1972?

# . . . Answers

678. Sun Yat-sen

679. Sandwich Islands

680. Tudor

681. El Salvador

682. Peter Stuyvesant

683. Puerto Rico Trench

684. Gallipoli

685. Madison

686. A spy

687. Katmandu

688. India

689. Chou En-lai

690) In which country is Transylvania?

691) King Boleslaus the Brave ruled where?

692) What Incan city high in the Andes was discovered by Hiram Bingham in 1912?

693) Which part of the newly formed Federation of Malaysia seceded in 1965?

694) What was the name of the 3rd century queen of Palmyra who conquered Syria, Mesopotamia and parts of Egypt?

695) Most famous street of Leningrad (St. Petersburg)?

696) Tito's full name?

697) What is the name of Japan's large northern island?

698) Who did Aaron Burr shoot in his Weehawken, N.J., duel in 1804?

699) Who explored the St. Lawrence River during 1534-41 and stopped at the future sites of Quebec Cty and Montreal?

700) Which Argentine president's wife was much loved by the urban masses?

701) What rocky headland's ownership is disputed by Britain and Spain?

# . . . Answers

690. Rumania

691. Poland

692. Machu Picchu

693. Singapore

694. Zenobia

695. Nevsky Prospekt

696. Josip Broz Tito

697. Hokkaido

698. Alexander Hamilton

699. Cartier

700. Eva (Evita) Perón

701. Gibraltar

702) What was the title of the chief magistrate of Venice?

703) What was the name of the 1904 alliance between Britain and France?

704) Alexander the Great's father?

705) At about what date did the Arabs invade Palestine?

706) Which cardinal was chief minister of Louis XIII and founded the French Academy in 1635?

707) What advocate of a Jewish state founded the World Zionist Organization?

708) When a volcano erupted in 1961, the population of what island in the South Atlantic had to be evacuated to Britain?

709) What was the name of the meeting place of the king's councilors in Westminster Palace which the Tudors turned into a criminal court?

710) Who was first secretary-general of the United Nations?

711) Besides the legendary twins, which of these was supposed to have founded Rome?
    a. Agamemnon          c. Aeneas
    b. Pericles           d. Archimedes

# . . . Answers

702. The doge

703. Entente Cordiale

704. Philip of Macedon

705. About 500 A.D.

706. Richelieu

707. Herzl

708. Tristan de Cunha

709. The Star Chamber

710. Trygve Lie

711. c

712) Port to Athens?

713) What French nobleman was involved in both the American and French revolutions?

714) What anti-British secret society founded by New York Irishmen in 1857 was named after an ancient band of warriors?

715) Highest point in the state of Hawaii?

716) Of the 2,084,000 U.S. troops that arrived in France for World War I, how many took part in active combat?
   a. 1,900,000
   b. 1,390,000
   c.   849,000
   d.   635,000

717) Who was the first child of English parents born in North America?

718) What state is known as the Bay State?

719) What position did Alexander Hamilton hold in George Washington's original cabinet?

720) What Shoshone woman guided Lewis and Clark on their explorations?

721) What hot wind blows onto southern Europe from the African deserts?

# . . . Answers

712. Piraeus

713. The Marquis de Lafayette

714. Fenians

715. Mauna Kea

716. b

717. Virginia Dare

718. Massachusetts

719. Secretary of the Treasury

720. Sacagawea

721. Sirocco

# QUESTIONS

722) Whose expedition circumnavigated the globe for the first time?

723) What year did Mussolini take power in Italy?
    a. 1922
    b. 1926
    c. 1928
    d. 1929

724) In 1903 the Russian Social Democrats split into what two parties?

725) When and where were the first slaves brought to North America?

726) Did the ancient Babylonians come before or after the Sumerians?

727) The Hanseatic League was a medieval alliance of cities where?
    a. northern Italy
    b. Hungary
    c. Spain and Portugal
    d. northern Germany and Holland

728) What is the name of the island colonized by the refugee mutineers of the HMS *Bounty?*

729) In which state is the Uncompahgre National Forest?

730) Year of great San Francisco earthquake and fire?

# . . . *Answers*

722. Magellan's, although he himself was killed on the way

723. a

724. Mensheviks and Bolsheviks

725. In 1619, to Jamestown, Va., by a Dutch ship

726. After

727. d

728. Pitcairn Island

729. Colorado

730. 1906

731) The 6th-15th century Khmer Empire ruled an area covered by which two present-day countries?

732) Where was Napoleon born?

733) On whose tombstone is this inscription?
*Author of the Declaration of American Independence, of the Statute of Virginia for religious freedom, and Father of the University of Virginia.*

734) Highest point in Washington state?

735) Who was the prime minister of Russia's provisional government overthrown by Lenin?

736) Jamestown and Plymouth were protestant colonies — what was the first English Catholic colony in North America?

737) State capital of Montana?

738) Which amendment to the U.S. Constitution lowered the voting age to 18, and when was it ratified?

739) What was the first war in which railroad transportation and the telegraph were widely used?

740) On what river is Paris built?

741) Spanish word for the New World conquerors?

# . . . Answers

731. Cambodia and Laos

732. Corsica

733. Thomas Jefferson's

734. Mount Rainier

735. Kerensky

736. Maryland

737. Helena

738. The 26th Amendment, ratified in 1971

739. The American Civil War

740. Seine

741. Conquistadores

742) Spanish fascist party that supported Franco?

743) Cambodia is the same size as:
   a. Colorado
   b. Missouri
   c. Ohio

744) Name the three big civilizations of ancient Mexico in the order in which they occurred.

745) "Deus vult" ("God wills it") was whose battlecry where?

746) State capital of Alaska?

747) In which state is the Allagash Wilderness Waterway?

748) When King Victor Emmanuel was made a gift of the newly liberated Sicily and Naples, he in return gave Garibaldi what symbolic gift?

749) Killer of Lee Harvey Oswald?

750) What Swedish city faces Copenhagen?

751) Who was described by Napoleon as "the bravest of the brave," was a leading member of the Old Guard, promised the king to bring Napoleon back to Paris in a cage, but instead joined forces with him and was tried and executed after Waterloo?

# . . . Answers

742. The Falange

743. b

744. Olmec, Zapotec, Maya

745. The Crusader knights in the Holy Land

746. Juneau

747. Maine

748. A sack of seedcorn

749. Jack Ruby

750. Malmö

751. Marshal Ney

752) Who was U.S. president between Warren G. Harding and Herbert C. Hoover?

753) What is the longest river in the world?

754) Which 20th century Irish revolutionary's American citizenship saved him from execution by the British?

755) British troops under what general were surrounded and forced to surrender at Saratoga in 1777?

756) State capital of New Mexico?

757) Who overthrew Madero in Mexico in 1913?

758) Year of the great fire in Chicago?

759) On what river is Lisbon built?

760) Who emerged as leader of the Parliamentarians in the English civil wars?

761) What was the name of the British prime minister who tried to appease Hitler at Munich?

762) Nicaragua is slightly larger than:
   a. Wisconsin
   b. New Hampshire
   c. New Mexico

763) Where was Buddha born?

# . . . Answers

752. Calvin Coolidge

753. Nile

754. De Valera's

755. Burgoyne

756. Santa Fe

757. Huerta

758. 1871

759. Tagus

760. Oliver Cromwell

761. Chamberlain

762. a

763. Southern Nepal, in the Himalaya foothills

764) What state is known as the Diamond State?

765) What Frenchman constructed the Suez Canal?

766) In which state is the Fort Peck Indian reservation?

767) What is the name of the second Watergate special prosecutor?

768) What is the name of the sea between Italy and Yugoslavia?

769) What Roman emperor abandoned Rome as capital of the empire?

770) Off which country is the Great Barrier Reef?

771) What 19th century American policy warned European powers not to interfere in Latin America?

772) What New York State commune was abandoned in 1879 but reorganized as a business two years later and survives today as a big corporation?

773) How long is the Alaska-Canada border?
   a. 1157 miles
   b. 1538
   c. 1702
   d. 1843

774) What state is known as the Buckeye State?

# . . . *Answers*

764. Delaware

765. Ferdinand de Lesseps

766. Montana

767. Leon Jaworski

768. Adriatic

769. Constantine the Great, who made Constantinople the capital

770. Australia

771. The Monroe Doctrine

772. The Oneida Community

773. b

774. Ohio

775) Home of Thomas Jefferson?

776) What was King Louis XIV of France known as?

777) Capital city of Bolivia?

778) What ancient Persian prophet introduced belief in the forces of good and evil, and reward or punishment after death?

779) Inactive volcano near Tokyo?

780) In 1250 the population of Europe was about:
   a. 23 million
   b. 45 million
   c. 70 million
   d. 110 million

781) State capital of Kansas?

782) Founder of British India?

783) Which large river forms the southern border of Oklahoma?

784) In 1935 Persia had its name changed to what?

785) Correct or incorrect?
   Kingdom of the Visigoths: Spain
   Kingdom of the Ostrogoths: Italy

# . . . Answers

775.  Monticello, Va.

776.  The Sun King (le roi soleil)

777.  La Paz

778.  Zoroaster

779.  Mount Fuji

780.  c

781.  Topeka

782.  Clive

783.  Red River

784.  Iran

785.  Correct

# QUESTIONS

786) What is the name of the large island that is part of the southern tip of South America?

787) What was the name of the unsuccessful revolt by liberal Russian military officers in 1825?

788) What was the protest called which was passed by the House of Commons on Nov. 22, 1641, and which listed the unconstitutional acts of the king?

789) Where in North America is the highest average rainfall?

790) What state is known as the Coyote State?

791) What was the first representative assembly in North America, elected in Jamestown, Va., in 1619, called?

792) Capital city of Sweden?

793) What was Frederick I of Prussia's "Tobacco Parliament"?
   a. a band of trained assassins
   b. a delegation of American Indians
   c. the assembled captains of the merchant fleet
   d. an informal gathering of political advisors

794) What two Allied scientific developments greatly increased German U-boat losses in World War II?

# . . . *Answers*

786. Tierra del Fuego

787. The Decembrist uprising

788. The Grand Remonstrance

789. Henderson Lake, British Columbia

790. South Dakota

791. House of Burgesses

792. Stockholm

793. d

794. Sonar and radar

795) Lebanon is slightly smaller than:
    a. Delaware
    b. Connecticut
    c. New Hampshire

796) What was the name of the conquering warrior kingdom in the interior of southern Africa that was organized and led by Shaka in the 1820s?

797) What was the popular name for F.D.R.'s legislation aimed at improving economic and social conditions?

798) What is the name of the sea passage between Vancouver Island and Washington state?

799) What British mathematician, philosopher and writer became one of the earliest antinuclear activists in his nineties?

800) Where is the world's highest town?

801) What was the name of the last British viceroy in India?

802) State capital of Virginia?

803) What were the names of the French general and British general killed in the British capture of Quebec?

804) Capital city of Morocco?

# ... Answers

795. b

796. Zulu

797. The New Deal

798. Juan de Fuca Strait

799. Bertrand Russell

800. Aucanquilcha, Chile

801. Lord Louis Mountbatten

802. Richmond

803. Montcalm and Wolfe

804. Rabat

805) What musical instrument did Frederick the Great of Prussia play?

806) Who were the leaders who signed the first SALT treaty in 1972?

807) What is the name of the part of Antarctica administered by New Zealand?

808) What was the dominant kingdom in Britain in the mid-7th century?

809) What was the 19th century term for the belief that the United States was meant to include the whole of North America?

810) What was the name of the large fleet destroyed by storms on its way to attack Elizabethan England?

811) Which is the only Central American country with no access to the Pacific?

812) What was the site of the first military engagement of the American Civil War?

813) Which has the greatest average depth, the Atlantic or Pacific Ocean?

814) In 1915 which Cunard ship was sunk off the southern coast of Ireland by a German submarine?

815) In which state is Lake Winnebago?

# . . . *Answers*

805. The flute

806. Nixon and Brezhnev

807. Ross Dependency

808. Northumbria

809. Manifest destiny

810. The Spanish Armada

811. Belize

812. Fort Sumter, Charleston, S.C.

813. Pacific

814. *Lusitania*

815. Wisconsin

816) Who was the most notorious traitor to the American side in the Revolution?

817) Capital city of Sri Lanka?

818) The East India Company made its fortune in the 1600s and 1700s exporting what from India?

819) What was the name of Mao's heir apparent who died on a flight to Russia?

820) San Marino is completely surrounded by what country?

821) Who was the first king of Hungary, later made a saint?

822) What was Howard Carter's big find in Egypt in 1922?

823) Where did Churchill make his "Iron Curtain" speech?

824) What year did St. Patrick begin missionary work in Ireland?
    a. 338
    b. 432
    c. 491
    d. 503

825) Who was elected British prime minister after World War II?

# . . . Answers

816. Benedict Arnold

817. Colombo

818. Hand-loomed cotton cloth

819. Lin Piao

820. Italy

821. Stephen

822. King Tut's tomb

823. Fulton, Mo.

824. b

825. Atlee

826) What is the name of the chain of islands stretching into the Pacific from Alaska?

827) What year did the Mormons settle in Salt Lake City?
    a. 1809
    b. 1814
    c. 1847
    d. 1856

828) Correct or incorrect?
    De Soto: Florida
    Coronado: Arizona

829) What is the name of Brazil's new capital in the undeveloped interior?

830) Syria is the same size as:
    a. Colorado
    b. Tennessee
    c. North Dakota

831) Which was founded first, Oxford or Cambridge University?

832) What was the name of the 1908 rebels against the Ottoman government who forced the sultan to restore a constitution?

833) What was the popular name for the regiment commanded by Ethan Allen?

# . . . Answers

826. Aleutian Islands

827. c

828. Correct

829. Brasilia

830. c

831. Oxford

832. The Young Turks

833. The Green Mountain Boys

834) During the 6th century, the Japanese began to adopt whose culture?

835) What is the line of latitude dividing North and South Korea?

836) Oil-rich sultanate under British protection on the island of Borneo?

837) At what gathering did Luther defend his teachings, resulting in his final break with Rome?

838) In what year did Khrushchev denounce Stalin at the Communist Party Congress in Moscow?

839) Small sea between the Aegean and Black Sea?

840) What event, on what date, is generally seen as the true beginning of the French Revolution?

841) Highest point in Idaho?

842) What is the name of the French Revolution's most intense period of bloodshed and confiscation?

843) Of the 6½ million people who had come to the New World by the 1770s, how many had come from Europe and how many from Africa?

844) What state is known as the Wolverine State?

# ... Answers

834. Chinese

835. The 38th Parallel

836. Brunei

837. The Diet of Worms

838. 1956

839. Sea of Marmara

840. The storming of the Bastille, July 14, 1789

841. Borah Peak

842. The Reign of Terror

843. From Europe, 1 million; from Africa, 5½ million

844. Michigan

845) What was the popular name of Teddy Roosevelt's Republican splinter group in the 1912 presidential election?

846) What strong cold dry northerly wind hits the French Mediterranean?

847) From what European country did Vasco da Gama set out on his voyages?

848) What Caribbean island is west of Barbados?

849) What city is on the Thames River in Connecticut?

850) What American was first to reach the North Pole, and in what year?

851) What Indonesian volcanic island exploded in 1883, sending dust into the atmosphere and tidal waves across oceans?

852) Where was Napoleon exiled the first time?

853) Highest point in Wyoming?

854) After the Bolsheviks had demobilized the imperial army, who organized the Red Army to fight the White Russians?

855) French founder of Quebec?

856) What state is known as the Cornhusker State?

# . . . Answers

845. The Bull Moose Party

846. Mistral

847. Portugal

848. Saint Vincent

849. New London

850. Peary, in 1909

851. Krakatoa

852. Elba

853. Gannett Peak

854. Leon Trotsky

855. Samuel de Champlain

856. Nebraska

857) On what river is Dublin built?

858) What was the only medieval banking center outside Italy?

859) Who led the British fascist blackshirts?

860) Amenhotep III was a famed ruler in what early civilization?

861) What fighting force was led by Walter the Penniless and Peter the Hermit?

862) The Pribilof Islands are part of what state?

863) In which state are the Blue Ridge Mountains?

864) What was Australia originally called by its European discoverers?

865) What was the name of the 1964 resolution passed by Congress that authorized presidential action in Vietnam?

866) What river flows from Lake Geneva into the Mediterranean?

867) What was the 1830 French uprising against Charles X and the ultraroyalists called?

868) Who was U.S. president between Martin Van Buren and John Tyler?

# . . . Answers

857. Liffey

858. Bruges

859. Oswald Mosley

860. Ancient Egypt

861. Part of the First Crusade

862. Alaska

863. Virginia

864. New Holland

865. Tonkin Resolution

866. Rhône

867. The July Revolution

868. William Henry Harrison

# QUESTIONS

869) What is the highest waterfall in the world?

870) What 19th century Irish leader lost support because of his involvement in a divorce case?

871) Which British general was defeated at Yorktown in 1781?

872) In which state are the Carlsbad Caverns?

873) Of what Alabama educational center did Booker T. Washington become head in 1881?

874) What small sea is a northern offshoot of the Black Sea?

875) What English king was overthrown by the Parliamentarians in the English civil wars?

876) What was the name of the Norwegian premier under Nazi occupation?

877) Who did the Athenian army defeat at Marathon?

878) State capital of Delaware?

879) Native Indians in British army?

880) What large river flows west to east across Nebraska?

# . . . Answers

869. Angel Falls in Venezuela

870. Parnell

871. Cornwallis

872. New Mexico

873. Tuskegee Institute

874. Sea of Azov

875. Charles I

876. Quisling

877. The Persians

878. Dover

879. Sepoys

880. Platte River

881) What country seized the U.S. merchant ship *May-aguez* in 1975?

882) What is the name of the sea between Greece and Turkey?

883) Of the 27 Roman emperors who reigned between 211 and 284, how many died violently?
    a. 0
    b. 5
    c. 8
    d. 23

884) On independence, British Honduras changed its name to what?

885) What is the popular name for the oath to secure a constitution taken by the French National Constituent Assembly a month before the Bastille was stormed?

886) What was the name of the commune that English idealist Robert Owen founded in 1825 in southern Indiana?

887) How long is the U.S.-Mexico border?
    a. 1432 miles
    b. 1545
    c. 1724
    d. 1933

888) What state is known as the Sooner State?

# . . . Answers

881. Cambodia

882. Aegean

883. d

884. Belize

885. The Tennis Court Oath

886. New Harmony Community

887. d

888. Oklahoma

889) Who was President Grant's able secretary of state?

890) Capital city of Peru?

891) What is the name of the ancient era dominated by Greek culture?

892) What state is known as the Bluegrass State?

893) The initial stage of the 19th century Indian Mutiny was the refusal of native-born soldiers to bite open cartridges because they were coated with what?

894) Which large river forms most of the northern border of Oregon?

895) Who led the 1952 army coup in Egypt and became its president?

896) What is the name of the strait ships use at the southern tip of South America?

897) Who led Haiti to independence?

898) What is the common name of the Catholic court used to try heretics, most often in Spain?

899) Where in Europe is the highest average rainfall?

900) State capital of South Dakota?

# . . . Answers

889. Hamilton Fish

890. Lima

891. Hellenistic era

892. Kentucky

893. Animal fats forbidden to Hindus and Muslims

894. Columbia River

895. Nasser

896. Strait of Magellan

897. Toussaint L'Ouverture

898. The Inquisition

899. Crkvice, Yugoslavia

900. Pierre

901) What individual bought Manhattan from the Indians, and in what year?

902) Capital city of Finland?

903) Maria Theresa of Austria and Hungary belonged to what dynasty?

904) What country's department of foreign affairs was officially titled until 1861 the Office for Barbarians?

905) What is the largest island off the western coast of North America?

906) What North American canyon is deeper than the Grand Canyon?

907) Who was the first prime minister of independent India?

908) What state is known as the Evergreen State?

909) What were the 1767 Townshend Acts meant to do in the New World?

910) Capital city of Nigeria?

911) Who fought against who in the Seven Years War?

912) Soviet answer to NATO?

913) What percentage of Norway is covered by forest?

# . . . Answers

901. Peter Minuit, in 1626

902. Helsinki

903. Hapsburg

904. China's

905. Vancouver Island

906. Hells Canyon on the Snake River

907. Nehru

908. Washington

909. Levy taxes

910. Lagos

911. France, Austria and Russia against Prussia aided by Britain

912. The Warsaw Pact

913. 25%

914) Name the five Great Lakes.

915) What is the term for the order maintained by the Roman empire during the first two centuries A.D.?

916) What is the name of the chain of islands between the Soviet Kamchatka Peninsula and Japan?

917) What Argentine-born Cuban guerrilla leader was killed in Bolivia in 1967?

918) What island is midway between Ireland and Britain in the Irish Sea?

919) What is the name of the British announcement in 1917 that Palestine should be a homeland for the Jews?

920) State capital of Wyoming?

921) In what building did George Washington bid farewell to his officers in 1783?

922) Capital city of Bangladesh?

923) What did India export to Britain in huge quantities in the 1700s that it imported in huge quantities from Britain in the 1800s?

924) Which UN secretary-general died in a plane crash in Africa?

# . . . *Answers*

914. Superior, Michigan, Huron, Ontario, Erie

915. Pax Romana

916. Kurile Islands

917. Che Guevara

918. Isle of Man

919. The Balfour Declaration

920. Cheyenne

921. Fraunces Tavern, New York City

922. Dacca

923. Cotton goods

924. Dag Hammarskjöld

# QUESTIONS

925) What is the official name of the tiny country of San Marino?

926) Who was the king of Denmark who became king of England in 1017?

927) Where is the gorge, and what is its name, in which some of humankind's earliest remains have been found?

928) Last emperor of Ethiopia?

929) What are the names of the two largest islands south of Cape Cod?

930) Sir Francis Drake's 1579 name for California?

931) What was the name of the American economic assistance plan for post-World War II Europe?

932) The Soviet Union covers what fraction of the world's land surface?

933) Because of their brilliant tents, Batu Khan's nomadic people where known as what?

934) What was the popular name for the reform wing of the 1840s New York Democratic Party, led by Martin Van Buren?

935) What was the name of the pilot of the American U-2 reconnaisance aircraft shot down over Russia in 1960?

# . . . Answers

925. Most Serene Republic of San Marino

926. Canute (Knut) II

927. Olduvai Gorge, Tanzania

928. Haile Selassie

929. Martha's Vineyard and Nantucket

930. New Albion

931. Marshall Aid Plan

932. One-sixth

933. The Golden Horde

934. The Barnburners

935. Gary Powers

936) British Crown Colony that China threatens to re-possess?

937) Who was head of a theocratic state in Geneva during 1541-64?

938) Straits at Gallipoli?

939) Highest point in Maine?

940) Highest point in Massachusetts?

941) Where was Napoleon exiled the second and final time?

942) State capital of Michigan?

943) What state is known as the Gopher State?

944) What is the world's oldest continually occupied city?

945) What was the greatest 15th century Italian banking family?

946) What Caribbean island is between Saint Lucia and Dominica?

947) What is the extreme southwestern tip of England called?

# . . . Answers

936. Hong Kong

937. Calvin

938. Dardanelles

939. Mount Katahdin

940. Mount Greylock

941. St. Helena

942. Lansing

943. Minnesota

944. Damascus, Syria

945. The Medicis

946. Martinique

947. Land's End

948) What was the name of the American intelligence ship seized by the North Koreans in 1968 and held for eleven months?

949) Islands off the extreme southwestern tip of England?

950) What was the name of the committee investigating J.F.K.'s assassination?

951) What is the name of the only active volcano on the European mainland?

952) What is the second highest mountain in the world?

953) State capital of Nebraska?

954) State capital of Nevada?

955) After Napoleon's defeat at Waterloo, the five crowned monarchs of what nations divided up Europe among themselves?

956) On what river is Hamburg built?

957) What state has the Painted Desert?

958) Where in America is the now transported London Bridge?

959) Mussolini seized what African nation in 1935?

# . . . Answers

948. USS *Pueblo*

949. Scilly Islands

950. The Warren Commission

951. Mount Vesuvius

952. K2 (Godwin-Austen)

953. Lincoln

954. Carson City

955. Austria, Russia, Prussia, France and England

956. Elbe

957. Arizona

958. Lake Havasu City, Arizona

959. Ethiopia

960) Abel Tasman discovered Tasmania and it became known as what?

961) What French river is famed for the chateaux along its banks?

962) Where is the famous Blue Grotto cavern?

963) Who held the pass at Thermopylae?

964) In which state is the Zuni Indian reservation?

965) What state is known as the Tar Heel State?

966) In what American city is the gothic skyscraper known as the Woolworth Building?

967) What state is known as Old North State?

968) Guadalcanal is in what island group?

969) What is the name for Nepalese-born soldiers in the British or Indian army?

970) State capital of Florida?

971) For how many days were 52 of the American hostages held in Iran?

972) State capital of Idaho?

973) In which state is the Dixie National Forest?

# . . . Answers

960.  Van Diemen's Land

961.  Loire

962.  Island of Capri, off Italy

963.  300 Spartans

964.  New Mexico

965.  North Carolina

966.  New York City

967.  North Carolina

968.  Solomon Islands

969.  Gurkha

970.  Tallahassee

971.  444

972.  Boise

973.  Utah

974) What country contains Serbia, Croatia and Montenegro?

975) What is the second largest lake in Nicaragua?

976) What state is known as the Beaver State?

977) What is the name of the Viking leader who reached North America about 1000 A.D.?

978) Capital city of Ecuador?

979) State capital of Kentucky?

980) How many separate forces had the British planned to field against the Americans at Saratoga?

981) Capital city of Colombia?

982) State capital of Louisana?

983) What river forms the border between Pennsylvania and New Jersey?

984) The Suez canal was nationalized by Egypt in what year?

985) What is the old regional name for the southern tip of South America?

986) What city did Britain gain from China as a result of the Opium War?

# . . . Answers

974. Yugoslavia

975. Lake Managua

976. Oregon

977. Leif Eriksson

978. Quito

979. Frankfort

980. Three

981. Bogotá

982. Baton Rouge

983. Delaware

984. 1956

985. Patagonia

986. Hong Kong

987) In which state is Mount Rushmore?

988) What state is known as the Volunteer State?

989) Capital city of Denmark?

990) What is the name of the largest lake in northern Utah?

991) Why did France have to withdraw from Canada in 1763?

992) Capital city of West Germany?

993) What bay has the world's highest tides?

994) State capital of Washington?

995) What are the Yugoslav alps called?

996) State capital of Oregon?

997) Where is the world's biggest meteor crater?

998) Capital city of Ghana?

999) Islands off the northern tip of Scotland?

1000) In which state is the Grand Teton National Park?

1001) Who was independent Kenya's first premier?

# . . . *Answers*

987. South Dakota

988. Tennessee

989. Copenhagen

990. Great Salt Lake

991. As a result of losing the French and Indian War against Britain

992. Bonn

993. Bay of Fundy, Nova Scotia

994. Olympia

995. Dinaric Alps

996. Salem

997. New Quebec, Canada

998. Accra

999. Orkney Islands

1000. Wyoming

1001. Jomo Kenyatta

1002) Capital city of Burma?

1003) Philip of Hesse and John Frederick I of Saxony led what 16th century league?

1004) Capital city of Zambia?

1005) In which state is Mount Rainier?

1006) Capital city of Thailand?

# . . . Answers

1002.  Rangoon

1003.  The Schmalkaldic League

1004.  Lusaka

1005.  Washington

1006.  Bangkok

# MORE THRILLING READING!